50 Things to Make with a Broken Hockey Stick

50 Things to Make with a Broken Hockey Stick

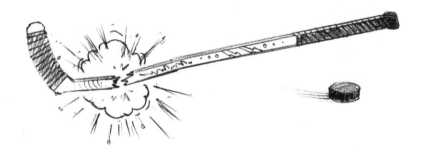

PETER MANCHESTER

GOOSE LANE

Edited by Rhona Sawlor.
Cover illustrations by Peter Manchester.
Cover design by Paul Vienneau.
Book design by Julie Scriver.
Printed in Canada by Transcontinental Printing.
10 9 8 7 6 5 4 3 2 1

National Library of Canada Cataloguing in Publication

Manchester, Peter, 1952-
    50 things to make with a broken hockey stick / Peter Manchester, author and illustrator.

Includes index.
ISBN 0-86492-358-9

    1. Hockey sticks — Humor. 2. Hockey sticks. 3. Canadian wit and humor (English) I. Title. II. Title: Fifty things to make with a broken hockey stick.

PN6231.H54M35 2002   C818'.602   C2002-903640-2

Published with the financial support of the Canada Council for the Arts, the Government of Canada through the Book Publishing Industry Development Program, and the New Brunswick Culture and Sports Secretariat.

Goose Lane Editions
469 King Street
Fredericton, New Brunswick
CANADA E3B 1E5
www.gooselane.com

To Sheelagh, who is supportive beyond reason

Table of Contents

Introduction

Skating on the first ice of winter, hockey stick in hand, makes a person feel like an artist gazing on a newly gessoed canvas: anything is possible. The most outrageous manoeuvres seem attainable, the season brims with possibilities. Sadly, gravity, dexterity, and a host of other factors chip away at our fantasy, and reality comes calling. All aspiring athletes feel the inequality between ourselves and the pros. Yet every last player in the NHL uses the same tools and equipment available to the local rink rat. Of course, the professional player's skates and stick might cost many hundreds of dollars, and the uniforms and padding are all customized and therefore very expensive. But every hockey player has a hockey stick that is much like everyone else's. Research shows that price is the number one factor in buying a hockey stick. Most of us are cheapskates (cheap-sticks?), but, no matter how much we pay, every stick can end up broken and discarded.

When a hockey player's exuberance on ice leads to the busting up of a hockey stick, and it is cast aside, seemingly worthless, a small thought balloon pops up. In the recesses of any hockey-obsessed brain, a premonition lurks: a broken stick is not trash. It has potential, unseen possibilities. As the gardens of hockey playing families will attest, broken sticks make great tomato stakes in the "rough sledding" months of summer, but take heed: they are a resource worthy of greater works.

The hockey stick has a spotty and colourful past. Theories vary as to who came up with the first one. Like anyone flummoxed by research, I have made up my own Eurocentric version, based on no research whatsoever, with apologies to the true pioneers. (For the real story, read *The Stick*, by Bruce Dowbiggin.)

Remember, if you will, that an ape threw a jawbone into the air in the movie *2001: A Space Odyssey*. You will no doubt remember that the jawbone did not have a good straight stick attached to it — it fell off and was lost in the final edit. Mr. Kubrick told me this with his last breath.

At some point in pre-history, jaw-bones of wild animals were certainly lashed to sticks, giving us a now-familiar form. Proto-humans knew it was good for something, but the world was new and rinks unfrozen. Eventually, a pastime developed as pre-historic man started whacking slap shots of wildebeest poop towards rival hominid troupes.

In an environment of such fun, a game would have eventually developed, with blue lines and penalty caves. If it had, spaceships might never have been invented, and pick-up games of a dusty hockey-like game would still be raging, played by australo-pithecines at Olduvai Arena.

Fast forward a few millennia to North Africa. Samson, biblical bully and legendary paramour, is looking for trouble. He has just soundly thrashed the Smithereens with "the jawbone of an ass." (Jawbone only, no stick mentioned.) This Old Testament high-boning would certainly put him in the penalty box of history under today's rules, but back then you got a bad haircut, you were disgraced by a column, the arena collapsed, the camera faded. If Samson had only been more adaptive with sporting equipment and had dallied less with Delilah, he would have found a good springy handle for his jawbone and waded into the hubbubs of ancient North Africa with unrivalled leverage. I have not found an Old Testament reference at the Hockey Hall of Fame, so I guess this line of research is still incomplete.

I will not dwell further on the many times throughout history that the hockey stick was almost invented. Such a useful tool I am sure exists in a nascent form in the sketches of Leonardo da Vinci. High in the suspending structures of Gothic Cathedrals lie flying buttresses that are strikingly similar to inverted hockey sticks. Accidental? Heck, no, those early architects were just thinking too big. Isaac Newton, had he devised the hockey stick, would have been hanging out in a not-very-

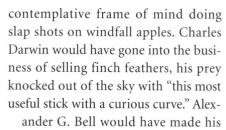

contemplative frame of mind doing slap shots on windfall apples. Charles Darwin would have gone into the business of selling finch feathers, his prey knocked out of the sky with "this most useful stick with a curious curve." Alexander G. Bell would have made his first phone call with the words, "Watson, come here. We need you in net."

These famous folks all lived and worked in places with balmy winters. It was not until humanity really lost its collective mind and moved way north and across oceans that the development of the hockey stick really got going.

As the building of sailing ships and the hunger for lumber slowly deprived North America of its tall, straight trees, our forefathers were left with skinnier and skinnier wood for the masts. Why, they were down to 1″ by ½″ stalks in those pre-metric days. In desperation one winter, as the ice glazed over a pond, a carpenter strapped on his skates and headed out to rough up his ice skating sibling with some lumber brought to him by a Mi'kmaw buddy. This wood he held in his hands was a stick he had used for swatting empty tuna cans, then called "paddies," about the workshop and into a fishing net. In the argot of the day, the activity was called "Mi'kmaq paddy whack." The brother of this carpenter was no slouch. With unexpected zeal, he presented his own tuna-can-smashing Mi'kmaq-supplied stick, and *voila*, they went out to get some more zeals on the ice. The Blood and Zeals concept was so successful it was adopted as a very profitable campaign by wildlife protection groups.

Unknown to most, the ultimate compliment has been paid to the hockey stick by NASA. Beneath the high-tech shell of the space shuttle lies a lattice work fabricated of finely laminated shafts of hard wood, stripped of gummy tape residue and wintry sweat — broken hockey sticks. Mysterious black vans would pick them up in the dead of night from the rinks' trash bins. This is why occasionally Canadian astronauts are invited aboard the shuttle, as their relationship with hockey sticks is more evolved than that of their cousins to the south. The pee-wee, midget, and bantam leagues gave rise to the space industry of today.

Pre-space-age hockey sticks were fabricated of fine wood. Reputations were made and lost on the selection of raw materials. The demands of industry and hockey were so great that soon the forests of North America were denuded of all the good wood, so the search was on for a suitable replacement. Leave it to those busybody ski fabricators in Finland to come up with the idea of laminating together lots of layers of wood and space-age resins. Cheap, flexible, and strong sticks could be made of this bogus wood. The research that goes into finding the best combination of natural and synthetic materials for the perfect hockey stick is staggering and ongoing.

For the craft projects in *50 Things to Make with a Broken Hockey Stick*, however, I ask my readers to use old-fashioned sticks with no aluminum or carbon. Wooden sticks flex a great deal under tension before breaking and are surprisingly strong. They are passed down through a hierarchy of siblings and neighbours and retain their shape and utility, until that fateful day when they fracture beyond the repairing abilities of duct tape and glue. At this point, they are tossed in a corner of the garage awaiting transformation.

Many uses of a broken hockey stick are obvious, as our countless tomato stakes can testify. In *50 Things to Make with a Broken Hockey Stick*, I strive to realize the full potential of this composite of resin and wood. My list is not complete, as the broken hockey stick is an almost infinite resource. My wish is to display the potential in the seemingly mundane and show you that you can make great stuff with them.

Any inspired project, at its inception, contains the potential of perfection. In its dream form, the project sits in an early morning haze, glowing with the first rays of the sun, a shining testament to one's creative and technical prowess. But the annoying realities — poor tools,

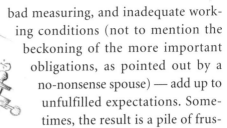

bad measuring, and inadequate working conditions (not to mention the beckoning of the more important obligations, as pointed out by a no-nonsense spouse) — add up to unfulfilled expectations. Sometimes, the result is a pile of frustration, set out for next week's garbage collection. Mistakes and misadventure do help you do things better the next time, though, so take heart.

Some projects require more hardware and tools than others. Know your abilities and limitations, ask for help if you need it — an inquiring trip to a neighbour often turns into an afternoon of laughs, beers, and borrowed tools. An astute reader sees that within this combination there lies danger. Working with wood is a timeless pastime, and most processes should not be rushed. So take your time, think things through, measure twice, cut once. I must also caution that proprietary information as to the actual makeup of a stick is not mine to be had. Examine the weirder combinations of components that make up your busted hockey sticks to see if they are suitable for the project at hand. Some sticks might just have to remain sticks.

The heartbreak of a terminal fracture of that favourite hockey stick could lead to a breakthrough in creativity and a good way to occupy your time until the ice returns. Use the sad remains to manufacture items for outdoors, items for indoors, and items with absolutely no purpose whatsoever. Why leave trash outside when you can bring it inside and call it a craft? Earn the admiration of your friends, praise from your family, and the grudging respect of strangers. You won't necessarily find easy, practical instructions in *50 Things to Make with a Broken Hockey Stick*, but you will never throw away another hockey stick once you've experienced the hours of fun you'll have attempting to complete these entertaining but questionable projects.

1. Ice Sail

When the icy gales of December blow, forget this hockey business. With broken hockey sticks and a garbage bag, you can fly across the ice like a paleo fun-seeker with his mammoth rib rig. If you have awning scraps, or, heaven forbid, you buy a length of sailcloth, your ice sail will last longer.

Make an A shape out of three pieces of broken stick, drill holes, and bolt them together. Keep the bolt ends facing away from you and cover them with duct tape. (A high speed encounter with metal parts can be unpleasant.) An extra cross piece near the point makes a useful handle and gives better balance under full sail. Use a staple gun to attach the awning fabric/sailcloth/garbage bag. If you are using a garbage bag, the copious use of duct tape is advisable along the stapled edges.

"Ice" is derived from the Sanskrit word for "smooth," according to author Wayne Grady. That is the kind of ice you want, and you will wear your skates. You'll be surprised how fast you'll go in a brisk wind. This experiment might have a Darwinian component, should you test the sail without first testing the ice. To avoid a frigid demise, stay off thin or bumpy ice, and remember that this sail will take you into uncharted territory quickly. Technique is up to you — just remember your tacks, jibe, scuppers, and poop decks, and you'll do fine.

2. Mock Moose

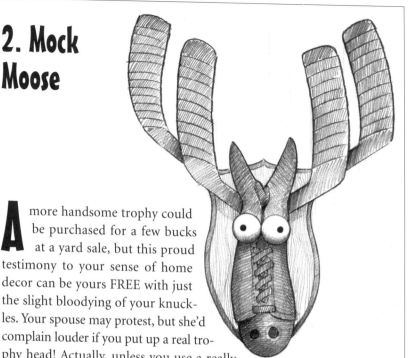

A more handsome trophy could be purchased for a few bucks at a yard sale, but this proud testimony to your sense of home decor can be yours FREE with just the slight bloodying of your knuckles. Your spouse may protest, but she'd complain louder if you put up a real trophy head! Actually, unless you use a really old skate, you might achieve a trophy with no animal content whatsoever, barring carelessness with your own body parts.

You'll need a skate, the blade ends of four sticks, two ping-pong balls, a mounting board, and plenty of black stick tape. Carefully slice down the back seam of the skate, and pull each side outwards to form the moose's ears. Tape these up to give them a good ear shape. For the antlers, cut the sticks so that the shafts are the same length, no more than 8" long. Cut the ends of the first two sticks at a slight angle so they fit together in a V. Find a scrap piece of stick. Holding the two antlers at the desired angle, pre-drill holes through them and the piece of scrap to make the brace that will hold the antlers in place.

Using a sharp utility knife, and cutting away from yourself, cut a hole the same size as the stick, about 3/4" x 1 1/8", out of each side of the heel. They should be the same height above the sole and the same distance from the heel support because you'll insert one stick into each to form the first tier of antlers. The cuts are tough to make, so take your time.

Insert the first two antlers through the holes in the skate and screw the rack together using the brace you've already made. Add the next tier of antlers by screwing these to the mounted ones. Attach them from the back with screws no longer than the combined thickness of the sticks. Theoretically, you could make a really big rack, but I stopped at a modest four-pointer.

For eyeballs, draw dots on the ping pong balls to give your beast the look you like. Slip pointy sheet rock screws no longer than the diameter of the ball through the top eyelets on the skate, and thread the ping pong balls right on to them. To keep the eyes close together, wrap a rubber band around the screws behind the eyes. Wrap black hockey tape from the heel support to the nearest blade brace. This will sort of look like the beast's neck.

Finding a suitable mounting board is up to you. I asked a qualified woodworker to cut one out for me. To make attaching the trophy to the plaque easier, he also ripped a groove the same width as the skate blade down the centre of the plaque on his table saw.

The collective whimsy of this project weighs a lot. Hold the skate to the board with a couple of mounting brackets, fastening them from the back of the plaque to maintain the trophy's elegance. Add a hanging bracket, mount it on the wall — better yet, mount several in a row — and give the neighbours something to talk about.

3. Catapult

The name alone strikes fear in the hearts of all cats. You, of course, will NOT launch cats. Your projectiles of choice are the foul apples of fall and the mouldy oranges found in the far recesses of the vegetable crisper. Maybe even trap-squished mice that you don't know how to dispose of. I won't go on about the dos and don'ts of Detritus (the Roman god of garbage), but what it's acceptable to hurl over your fence is a standard to which only you are privy. (Don't hurl stuff from the privy.)

You will need a good length of hockey stick (the longer and more flexible, the farther the delivery), a length of two-by-four for the base, some wood scraps, a couple of eye hooks, some strong cord and a nail for the release mechanism, an old kitchen strainer, and some hockey tape.

To start, you might consider a taper cut along the length of the stick to give it more spring. From about the middle of the stick, draw a line along the broad side towards one end, aiming for about a 1/4" width at the tip. Cut carefully along this line. The most important part of this project is the base. It must hold the end of the stick firmly, and it is subject to the greatest stress. See my diagram for bracing, but if you have a better idea, go for it.

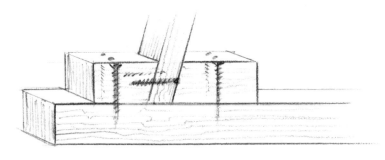

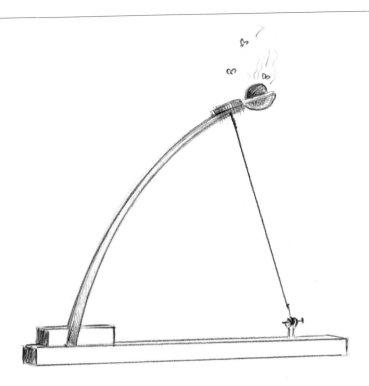

For the basket to hold the payload, strap an old hand-held kitchen strainer to the stick with hockey tape. Traditionally, catapults were mounted on wagons, and adding a wheel assembly to your catapult could intimidate adversaries and get a nod of admiration from peers. The catapult of old also had a winding device to bend it, with a ratchet to hold the tension. Since you are not storming castles, however, you can simply bend yours down and hook it on to the trigger device made of eye hooks and a nail. Drive the eye hooks into the base about 2" apart. Tie one end of the cord to the business end of the catapult, and tie the nail to the other end of the cord, which has been cut just long enough to create sufficient tension for a good launch. Slip the nail through the eye hooks so it's ready to be yanked out when you yell, "Ready! Aim! Fire!" This puppy whips up pretty fast, so pay attention when using it. Keep the small kids away, and don't hurl heavy objects in an unsafe manner. The use of this catapult is an outdoor activity.

4. Pasta Dryer

Here is a use for a busted hockey stick never envisioned in the pioneering days of high-impact ice sports. To make pasta, you need a big slab of marble and some flour, eggs, salt, and water. You also need a lot of time, wine, and either strength with a rolling pin or one of those pasta rolling gizmos. It is a lot of work, but it is also a very social activity.

Of course, you'll need a stick on which to hang your pasta to dry. A busted hockey stick. That's all. What, you thought I was going to tell you something special? You need a long straight piece of wood, cleaned of spit, polish, hockey tape, and all other unidentifiable schmutz. Now, you might easily reach for a broom handle, but this approach would be misguided. You see, you are in the act of making pasta. You could have simply chosen to go to the local market and buy fresh pasta, but you didn't. You are reading a book describing many dubious uses for a broken hockey stick. You need to go through the process. Clean up the stick, rub in some flour, place it over the backs of two chairs, and hang your strips of pasta to dry. Ta-dah! Resourceful as ever, you have transformed a fractured hockey stick into a highly-functional culinary accessory.

5. Piñata Stick

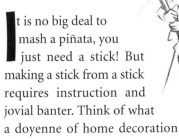

It is no big deal to mash a piñata, you just need a stick! But making a stick from a stick requires instruction and jovial banter. Think of what a doyenne of home decoration whose initials are M.S. and whose name rhymes with Mithra Stirrup would do. You need to adorn your stick with bright, festive colours. Wrap it in crepe paper. Give it streamers. Listen for mariachi music in the wind, cue the happy kids in white cotton shirts with brilliant sashes and huarache sandals.

The piñata itself you can construct using the traditional balloon and papier maché method. Be sure to put a few loops of string around the balloon for a hanging device as you are laying on the papier maché. This vessel is in for some pounding, so lay it on thick if the age group of *destructeros* is over double digits. Be creative with shapes, bright paper, and presentation.

Any situation involving a blindfolded individual wildly swinging a reborn hockey stick at a moving target calls for some ground rules and someone to keep back the crowd eager to pick up the goodies loosed from the piñata. As adult entertainment, nothing goes better with summer libations than a good, competitive spirit blindly smashing away at an elusive target.

6. Firewood Holder

The wooden firewood holder is an outstanding post-modern deconstructionist statement: wood in one form supporting wood in another form. A cradle and its logs: one we allow to be consumed by a warming flame, the other we choose to preserve as structure. Both began as similar stands of trees. One was crudely cut and split, while its brother in arbourdom was finely hewn, shaped, and transformed to an item of utility. Each might just as easily have become the other. By what measure were these two fates determined?

Who cares? This firewood holder has a distinctive look that whispers "broken hockey sticks, used in a silly excuse for recycling." Yes, there is that way of looking at it, but don't you still see your elementary school art projects proudly displayed at your mom's house even though you are now in your forties? Uphold that fine tradition. Make this firewood holder and give it to her! It is practical and has a certain oriental aesthetic.

Using my illustrations and your imagination, come up with your own plans for this handy item. So long as the side pieces are all one length, and the bottom pieces match, and the joints are sturdy, you'll be happy with the results.

Alternatively, you could make a magazine rack. The curious similarity to the firewood holder is strictly a coincidence. You see, this magazine rack holds yet another form of wood, pulp fibre, transformed into a nearly

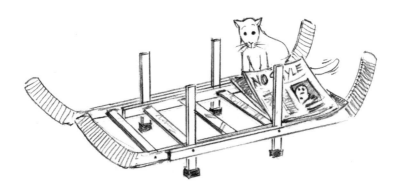

two-dimensional sheet. Yes, it does have the same beautiful lines as the wood rack in profile, but this magazine rack also sports several dividing posts so that you can systematically move your journals and publications from the right to the centre and then to the left. An observant spouse will assume these journals are being read when you are actually practicing the ancient domestic art which the Romans called *transit cumulare*. I am of the species *homocumulare*, one who makes piles. The fastidious polar opposite is the *homomunde*, a "tidy person" or spouse. There is a theory among seismologists that the reason the West Coast suffers so many earthquakes is that more of the residents tend to accumulate heavy, glossy magazines. The sheer weight of these collections causes the continental shelf to fracture. You need not subject this rack to such stress since it is just made of broken hockey sticks, but a few well-chosen publications in it next to your favorite chair will enhance any domestic relaxation time.

7. Beach Chair

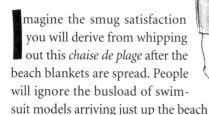

Imagine the smug satisfaction you will derive from whipping out this *chaise de plage* after the beach blankets are spread. People will ignore the busload of swimsuit models arriving just up the beach as they crowd around you and your chair, deep in admiration.

Fabric selection is crucial. You need a tough cloth, such as canvas, that will withstand the elements at the beach. Choose a fabric with a colourful pattern that will hide the sweat absorbed from your back or the splotch of goo that greases your bod as you lounge on the beach.

This chair begs for modification to fit your individual tastes and size. Using measurements that fit the end user (so to speak), cut two stick pieces to the same length for the back, cut two more for the seat, and cut four or five crosspieces as you choose and corner braces if you want to get fancy. Cut two canvas pieces wide and long enough to make a comfortable sling for the seat and back, allowing extra length for folding the edges over the frame. Staple the fabric securely across the frame by bringing it to the inside, using lots of 3/8" staples. Hinge the back and seat together (hinges should be salt resistant — brass is good), and finish the project off by securely attaching a strip of nylon webbing to each side for stability. The bracing is important, as the twists, shifts, and stretches of beach lounging can put a lot of stress on a chair.

8. Doll Cradle

Many parents wish nothing more for their children than that they grow up to be professional hockey players. After all, infants naturally display many of the qualifications. They spit and drool a lot, fart without remorse, take what they want, and are transparently emotional. Stick handling and skating can be picked up as they grow. But nothing prepares Baby for the NHL like a hockey-themed cradle. It rocks gently, mimicking the subtle jostling of team members on the bench, and its shape is not unlike the box that really tough hockey players spend a fair amount of time in. Wait a minute. You'd put your child in a cradle made of hockey sticks? Infants squirm way too much, they climb, they explore. Get a real crib. Use this for dolls and teddies.

It is easy to construct. The box is made of hockey stick slats that are sanded and glued together. The rockers are made out of blades with the heel sanded down to a nice curve and attached end-to-end. Splice the rocker pieces together by using a scrap piece of stick screwed across the joint from the back. Mount support struts on the box and attach the blades as shown in the illustration. Make sure that there are no protruding screws — you don't want to injure your future All-Star. Stick some team logos on the cradle so playtime becomes an opportunity for baby to absorb the iconic importance of team names like "Georgian Bay Giblets" or "Pickwaucket Pencil Pointers."

9. Sundial / Snow Depth Gauge

A sundial can be useful even if the sun isn't shining. As a snow depth gauge, it will tell you how much work is required to shovel off the pond for the next hockey game. Your sundial / snow depth gauge might even be buried in snow up to the wagungas. But knowing how high up your wagungas are makes for easy calibration. Sunlight gets scarce in the winter, and you probably won't be running out to see what time it is when it's 30 below anyway. It's time to be inside, carving and sanding that beautiful sundial gizmo.

Carve an elegant spire, handsomely crafted from a hockey stick with the care that only somebody with too much time on his hands can give. The needle of the sundial needs to come to a nice point. You also need a dial. This need not be a full circle because the sun isn't available to cast a shadow around a full circle anyway unless you live where you regularly catch Arctic char and have to watch your back for polar bears when you go to the dump. And while you are at the dump, why not look for a wall clock that is fixable and just give your sundial contraption to that bear to use as a toothpick.

The sundial will not give you a very precise time, but you will get readings to within the hour. "Setting" your sundial will have to be done over a period of a whole year. Here's how. Those of us who are up to see the sun rise observe that the point at which it creeps over the horizon changes dramatically between summer and winter. These points are most divergent at the solstices, and the mid-point occurs at the spring and autumnal equinoxes. Take your readings at the equinox. This will give you an average of shadow positions for the rest of the year. Get a circle of cardboard and place the stick vertically in the centre. Draw a line along the centre of the stick's shadow at each increment of time you wish to be able to read: 6 AM, noon, 6 PM, whatever times you like. You can transfer this information to the permanent base that you'll make for your sundial.

For that, how about "borrowing" a hubcap from a meddlesome neighbor's car? Fill the inside with concrete, and, as it hardens, put a bolt in the centre with the threads facing up. Place odd bits of hockey sticks in the cement (or draw in it with a stick), copying the shadow increments you recorded at the equinox. Pre-drill up the center of the bottom of hockey stick, and when the cement hardens, screw it down onto the base. Make sure you place your masterpiece with the same orienation as when you took the original readings. And, remember the hubcap appropriation if you ever have that neighbour over for a garden party.

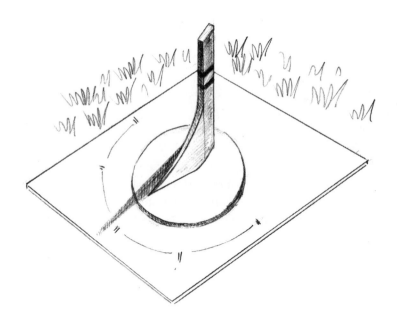

10. Curtain Rod

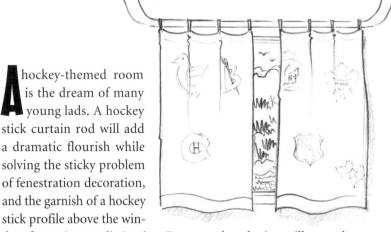

A hockey-themed room is the dream of many young lads. A hockey stick curtain rod will add a dramatic flourish while solving the sticky problem of fenestration decoration, and the garnish of a hockey stick profile above the window frame is very distinctive. Future archaeologists will marvel at your ingenuity, but the neighbours might call the zoning people or the fashion police should you fail to do this with panache. Unless you're a good hand with a sewing machine, you will need to recruit other domestic forces to sew extra big loops on the curtains to fit over the hockey stick rod.

To get the rods to fit the window will take some measuring and cutting. If you need more length on the broken sticks, you might splice the sticks from behind with a metal plate. It is often helpful to use a piece of dowel to join two pieces of wood end-to-end, although, simple as it seems, lining up the drilled holes and the dowel can be humbling. You need to be dead-on in you measurement and drilling to avoid those "I told you you're no carpenter" looks. The more streamlined technique may be to cut the pieces on a bias and take the glue/clamp route.

Installing this curtain rod can create a slight difficulty because they are top-heavy. This small problem with gravity and balance can be solved by using L hooks. Screw them into the window frame and drill holes in the rod base to accept the uprights. The rod will not tip or rotate if this is done properly.

11. Back Scratcher

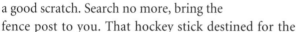

We are born with areas on our bodies that are nearly inaccessible to ourselves. At times, we are not unlike large bovines looking for the nearest fence post for a good scratch. Search no more, bring the fence post to you. That hockey stick destined for the kindling pile can be brought back from the brink of carbonization.

You might be tempted to just grab the ol' stick and start scratching, but the most satisfying store-bought backscratchers are those plastic monkey-paw numbers. Their popularity may lie in the subconscious connection to our simian ancestors' grooming habits. The author Robin Dunbar associates language development with the observation that much of primates' social bonding is maintained through communication of sounds. He surmises that gossip is an extension of the grooming ritual. Fussing over each other is a social activity, actually finding bugs in the fur is secondary.

I suggest that if you decide to make a back scratcher, you go beyond the simple hockey stick blade. A rake-like shape mimics the hand for a satisfying scratch, so get a bunch of blades and trim them with acute angles of equal profile to get a radiating pattern. Matching curves make this a better scratcher. Keeping the blades centered on the main stick, glue, clamp, and screw them together. The rough ends can catch and blemish finer fabrics, so sand where you can. But, if you are a t-shirt wearing TV-watching slob, don't worry about it.

12. Luge

DEADLY CHASM AHEAD

Luge is French for "bone-breaking device that scares the piste out of you." Theoretically, it's intended for the serpentine downhill courses you see in the Olympics. I can't help you out with the spandex outfits, but this sled looks like those sleds if you squint.

The traditional way to build a wooden luge involves steaming the runner pieces to a beautiful curve. This is certainly doable and makes a beautiful form. But let's just call this "the road not taken." A hockey stick with the blade still attached works just fine, with one small adjustment. Most sticks have a slight corner at the heel that must be sawn or sanded off, forming a smooth curve from shaft to blade. Two sticks of the same model and length, one right-handed and one left, are ideal.

Ultimately, this luge will require a whole hockey team's supply of busted sticks. Construction will be easiest if you begin with the sides. Cut two pieces (A) the length of the seat and five pieces (B) about 6" long for each side. (You will need 10 pieces the length of the seat, so you might as well cut them all at once.) Attach these (A and B) at the ends, the centre, and at 2/5 and 4/5 the length of the long piece. Pre-drill your holes using a bit for recessed screw heads so that, when the screws are fully screwed in, they are flush with the wood. Screw and glue the parts together, one screw per joint. Cut 5 pieces the width of the sled — about 14" — and attach them to the five vertical pieces of the sides. Now you have the framework to support the seat. To increase stability, cut two braces and attach them from the bottom of the centre piece of each side to the centre point of the seat supports. Use the longest possible screw as these braces take a lot of stress. Space the other six sticks evenly along the top of the seat and glue and screw them in, recessing the screw heads.

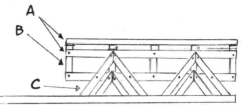

There is a reason why this bench you have just made is not attached directly to the runners: the sled would be too stiff. Give it some flexibility by attaching the runners with diagonal braces (C). It is important to cut these braces so they fit tightly and cleanly together. You will need 8 longer and 8 shorter pieces. Cut all the longer and all the shorter sticks identically, the same length and at the same angle. Attach these braces to the seat with screws, making sure that the bottoms line up to fit cleanly on the runners. The longer braces should be attached to the top and lower side sticks of the seat. Next, attach the runners to the diagonal braces. Pre-drill the screw holes and use the longest possible screws. You are now the proud owner of a luge.

This luge will perform in direct proportion to the care you use in making it, although it is not capable of withstanding jumps and "whumps." A heavy application of candle wax on the runners will give a faster ride. This is not a deep snow luge; it's for those icy, crusty hills of late winter. It will also do well being pulled by someone on skates. If you need a pull cord, attach it to the front of the seat, not to the runner blades. Of course, you could just use this luge as a coffee table that trips people up with its curious projections.

13. Book Ends

You might be using your bookshelf for other things besides books: a place to organize your eight-track tapes or the Mullet Cards from your Hockey Haircut Hall of Fame collection. But a lovely pair of hand-made bookends will display your books vertically so that you have to crane your neck and tilt your head to see the titles. Once you've made the basic bookends, you can customize them with flourishes that speak of your individuality, your creativity, your maniacal obsessions.

Since wood does not break in a straight line, you will need to cut some sticks into similar lengths. Then join the pieces together by gluing and clamping. First join two pieces for the base, and two more pieces for the uprights, creating four blocks of wood. Using more glue and a few screws, join two blocks at right angles to create each bookend. A quick pass with a table saw to trim all the edges straight would save lots of sanding time. No table saw? You can get nifty hand saws used for mak -ing mortice joints that cut nice and straight.

Now comes the creative part. You have a void to fill in that 90° space you created when making the book ends. In the parlance of *artistes,* this is "negative space." Your mission is to fill it with some memento, as tacky as possible, and place it in a Feng Shui kind of way so it fits that L perfectly. Where to get your ideas? A zen approach would be to visualize a mountain pool with reflections of serenity, clouds, mist, but this is hockey! You need to visualize a broken-down trailer in the woods, buried half-tires painted a festive white surrounding a dried-up flower bed. The TV is on inside, the Leafs vs. the Frostbacks. A big bowl of fried pork rinds is on the coffee table, which is missing a leg. A faded print of dogs playing pokeris on the wall. The fridge holds nothing but beer. Are you there yet? Now look on top of the fridge. Is there some knickknack suitable for your bookend space? That's exactly what you are looking for. If you are making bookends out of hockey sticks, chances are you have that perfect decoration right there in the room with you.

14. Travois

The long haul from car to rink to changing room and back to the car can be arduous. Ancient North Americans solved this problem by developing the travois. On it, they would haul their kids' kit bags from coulee to coulee without the aid of wheels, often harnessing their dogs to pull it. Now that would make a grand entrance to your next practice! This travois is collapsible, holds a good load, and will surely make others talk about you as your kids drag their stuff across the parking lot, noisily and with panache.

To put a travois together, you will first need to select your beast of burden. If it is you, a harness is not required — your hands will do. A four-footed friend will require a belt around the midriff with an attachment on each side to fasten the sticks to it. This harness can be devised from duct tape and an old belt.

You'll need two long lengths of stick for the sides of the travois and a couple of crosspieces between them to support the load. Attach the crosspieces by drilling holes and inserting bolts that have lock nuts on them, but leave the bolts loose enough that the pieces can still swivel and fold. Even if you don't have a dog or a pony, this gizmo can really save your back. You carry only a fraction of the weigh of your load of hockey (or fertilizer) bags, while the travois carries the rest.

15. Key Holder

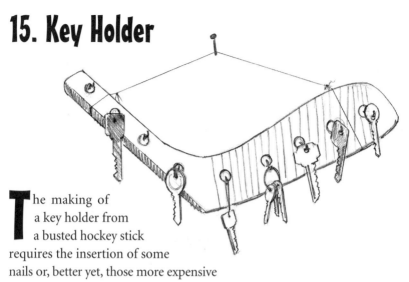

The making of a key holder from a busted hockey stick requires the insertion of some nails or, better yet, those more expensive brass hooks with an elegant skirt thingamabob that you see only on key holders. An entire industry exists to make those screw-in brass wafer-and-hook units for shop classes around the world. My mother still has a key holder I made decades ago, so do a good job, line up those nails or hooks well; this is going to have your name on it for a long time.

A post-modern version would consist of a nice straight piece of hockey stick with simple titanium rods sticking out. A Dadaist would randomly put in nails of various sizes after glueing all manner of hockey related printed material (game ticket stubs, programs, newspaper clippings) all over the stick. A deconstructionist would still be thinking, "What the heck is a straight piece of wood, anyway?" You, however, can do whatever you like. You could even make the key holder out of the blade part of the stick with your photo from your Pee Wee Hockey days varnished right onto it, next to a hand-written, heart-melting line saying something like, "Thanks for driving me to the rink all those years." You won't get encouragement for such mush here, but this is your hockey stick key holder, so embellish away!

16. Canoe Paddle

A good canoe paddle can set you back big bucks, but a person in a hurry can make one for nothing. Just cut off the end of a broken goalie stick — you'll have a funky paddle about 3 1/2" wide. Make two, join the shafts with duct tape or screws, and you've got a kayak paddle. If you're not in a hurry, though, you can make a nice one that will cost you nothing but a lot of sweat, some glue, and a friend with the appropriate tools.

The shape and dimensions of paddles are as varied as the . . . as the . . . well, the simile escapes me now, but there are a heck of a lot of styles. How do you select the one that's best for you? Go to your local boat shop and chat up the salesman. Act enthusiastic. Request a catalogue with photographs of the models available, and bada bing! Go home, carefully copy the shape you've selected, and make a pattern out of cardboard.

All paddles have the same general properties: a centre stick the length of the paddle, flanked by two pieces of stick on each side for the blade. These five pieces, joined side to side, will make a paddle about 6" wide. Determine your personal paddle length by holding your arms out at your sides and measuring palm to palm. The length of the blade depends on the paddle style, but a standard blade length would be 20".

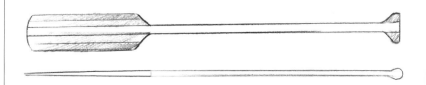

A paddle blade is usually thicker at the centre and tapers to about 1/4" at the edges.

Make friends with someone who has a joiner and band saw. The joiner will shave the sides very smooth for gluing, and the band saw will be handy for shaping the blade profile to save sanding time and effort. Glue the paddle pieces together with a waterproof glue or epoxy. Clamp tightly and let dry thoroughly. Use a belt sander to smooth out the blade and get it close to the final shape. Going from coarse to fine grit, sand the blade to as smooth a finish as possible.

To make the blade stronger and more durable, put on a layer of fibre-glass cloth using epoxy resin and hardener. Marine

AREA TO BE CUT OR SANDED AWAY

PADDLE ENDVIEW

resins make a nice finish on a paddle. This stuff is toxic, so follow instructions carefully. Sand the shaft and top handle perfectly smooth. The time you spend now making the handle fit comfortably will pay off handsomely later in smooth, blister-free strokes. If you refrain from paddle abuse, you will save yourself many hours of thinking, "Why didn't I just buy a stinking paddle in the first place?"

17. Walking Stick / Remote

Before the groans even start about yet another obvious straight stick project given a highfalutin' name, let me say right now, this is a very difficult project. It requires a straight stick AND a drilled hole. Not only that, you have to find a string for a handle grip. I am sorry to throw all these technical terms at you, but this is a how to book, and sometimes you just have to be specific. The proper walking stick should be about shoulder height with an ergonomically shaped hand grip. This means whittling down the corners and adding a little hockey tape for a good grip.

You can get a double-ended screw, but a hardware store would call it a double-threaded thingamabob. Install it at the business end of your walking stick. Pre-drilling the hole helps in this installation. This will give you a good point to jab into the ground along the trail and will cut down on the wear and tear on the wood. It will also inflict nasty wounds on unprotected feet and imagined predators.

One could get creative and sand down the shaft of the stick, whittle some cool designs, maybe paint on a stripe and throw on some feathers, but we are far from the days of merit badges and moms who praise any craft no matter how esthetically suspect. What you do for decoration is a testimonial to your personal identity. A collection of these sticks by the front door, propping up a well-worn hat, and perhaps a water bottle placed on a nearby table will fool everyone. Don't forget the dusty hiking boots casually set by aforementioned table, a well-thumbed John Muir book, and binoculars, perhaps.

Thanks to an accident of parallel evolution, this walking stick may also be used as a remote TV channel changer. It operates from any distance equal to the combined length of your arm and the stick and requires no batteries. It is strongly suggested that you change channels with a neutral disposition, as emotions and buttons seem to have an unsuccessful relationship and you might omit the screw on the end. This channel changer is way harder to lose than those darned little hand-held gizmos, but when the kids start fighting over it, your housewares should start getting nervous. There is just something about idle minds and channel surfing that brings out the rascal in all of us. So, if a fight is threatening to break out, maybe the kids should use this stick for its original purpose and get outside for a walk.

18. Quilt Stand

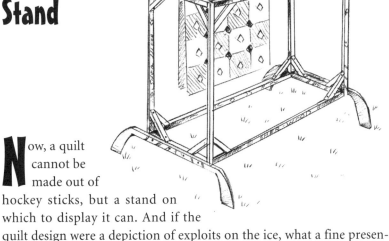

Now, a quilt cannot be made out of hockey sticks, but a stand on which to display it can. And if the quilt design were a depiction of exploits on the ice, what a fine presentation that would be. An ensemble of sorts.

The height of the quilt stand depends on the size of the quilt to be displayed. A double or queen-sized quilt would call for a structure about waist-high. You will need four pieces of the same length for the horizontals, and the same for the verticals. You can glean from the illustration that the uprights need some bracing. Cut all the braces the same length, with a 45° slant cut on each end, angled towards each other. You will need 16 of them, eight each for the top and bottom. Be sure to use clamps, screws, and glue for strength and stability when putting this stand together. When you have the box built, add the blade legs, fastening them to the bottom struts on each side. You need four blades of identical size and shape, or at least blades that have been modified so that they rest flat on the floor and the stand is level. This quilt stand could be an heirloom or a hairball — your craftsmanship will decide.

19. Wind Block

This project is a real no-brainer. You'll need five broken hockey sticks at least 40" long, some scrap pieces for stakes, and three yards of fabric. Choose a distinctive design that symbolizes your nature, your taste, and your love of hockey. Not only will this device protect you from blowing sand, but by displaying the fact that you own five busted hockey sticks, it will keep away the beach bullies, too.

Trim one end of each stick to a point for easy insertion in the ground at set-up time. Lay out the fabric and evenly space the sticks about every 24", allowing about 6" of extra fabric on each end for wrapping around the end sticks. Arrange the fabric so that there is room at the top of each stick to attach a length of cord. Staple the fabric to the sticks from what will be the windward side, using 3/8" staples about every 6" down the sticks. Attach about 6' of cord to the top of each stick, making a groove around the stick to prevent the string from slipping. To the other ends of the strings, attach ground stakes made out of scrap stick pieces whittled to a point (long stakes for soft sand, shorter ones for hard turf). This will provide the stability you need on blustery days. Set-up is simple: unfurl your masterpiece, drive the sticks into the ground, and tie them down with the ground stakes. Fun in the sun ensues.

20. Bathroom Accessories

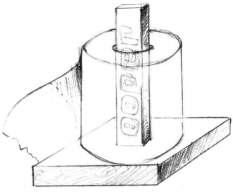

You knew darn well it had to come to this: the most basic daily function accomplished with the aid of a hockey stick.

As anyone who has visited a cabin with an outhouse knows, the paper holder has several forms. The most basic version is a neatly bound old retail catalog with dog-eared glossy pages. One step above this is the single-post style roll holder. It offers easy access to real toilet paper and no-hassle roll replacement. This style sidesteps the "roll towards you or away from you" debate currently raging in Home Decor circles.

What can I tell you about a stick attached to a board? You can challenge yourself by trying to cut out a perfectly round base. Or you might try an elaborate base of complex pieces fitted together with such skill that it will hold a captive audience's attention for the time required to take care of business. You might carve *The Thinker* at the end of the stick. Whatever you decide, just make sure that the stick is tall enough to actually hold the roll.

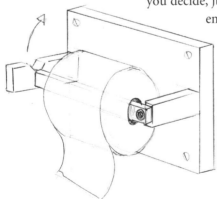

The conventional horizontal roll holder is a real craft project. A father could spend hours of quality time working on it with his child, passing on the proper use of tools, anecdotes of times past, and bathroom humour.

The most demanding part of this model is the bar. So the bar

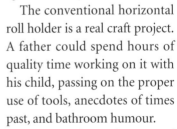

will rotate easily, drill a hole wider than the barrel of the screw you will use, but smaller than the head, into the end of one bracket. Drive the screw through one end of the bar, making sure it protrudes far enough to slip into the hole you drilled in the bracket. Cut a notch into the other arm of the bracket so that the paper holder falls easily and securely into place. Some toilet paper rolls are bigger than others, so give yourself one and a half times the radius of a new roll for proper clearance.

And since we're in the neighbourhood, how about ensuring your privacy in the privy with a lovely hand-crafted Witty Hockey Themed Bathroom Occupancy Designator, or WHTBOD?

You may choose any clever word combination to signify "occupied" and "unoccupied." George Maciunas coined the word "fluxus" in a lecture at a New York art gallery in 1961 to describe numerous activities and noises occuring simultaneously with an open-ended outcome. Sound like your bathroom in the morning? Another intellectual avenue is "zeitgeist," colloquial German for "what's in the air?" Just remember, the W in WHTBOD stands for Witty.

This is a simple yet elegant design. The curve of the hockey stick blade swings out nicely for an easily adjustable pointer. Simply screw the shaft of the blade to your mounting board, leaving enough leeway to position the pointer freely.

21. Washtub Bass

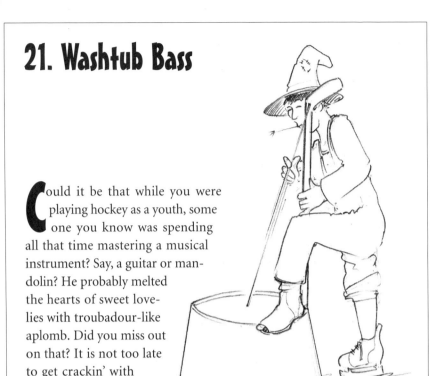

Could it be that while you were playing hockey as a youth, some one you know was spending all that time mastering a musical instrument? Say, a guitar or mandolin? He probably melted the hearts of sweet lovelies with troubadour-like aplomb. Did you miss out on that? It is not too late to get crackin' with something so basic that all you need is an old washtub, some strong twine, and a broken hockey stick. Generations of bluegrass lovers have mastered the technique of the washtub bass, so there is a possibility you could also.

This instrument uses an upturned washtub as a large resonator, with a string attached to a bolt at the centre of the tub and then fastened securely to the top of a stick about 60" long, the base of which is resting on the rim at the outside edge of the washtub. If you cut a notch in the stick, it will stay put, held in place with the tension of the string. Pulling back on the stick, thereby increasing the tension, will raise the tone, loosening the stick will lower the tone. Take the handles off the tub so they don't rattle with the vibrations. A washtub bass also tends to slide around a lot, but a no-slip platform will fix that problem.

Before you head out into the world with your new instrument, you might be well advised to practice a bit to recorded music. Low frequencies travel well, so you will be heard as you play. You might as well make those huge goofs in the privacy of your own home in front of only family members. As you improve, take your washtub bass to work and practice at coffee breaks. Join the washtub bass chat rooms on-line and download the tablature to "In the Pines." Keep at it, don't give up. When you hear those breakaway washtub solos on the radio, turn up the volume, hear the nuance, feel the groove.

Memorize the phrase, "Uh, is that in D?" That's all you need to know to join a bluegrass ensemble. Nod your head in time to the music and get a corncob pipe. For best effect, close your eyes and wave your head side to side with an exaggerated "I feel it now" posture. Hunch your shoulders like Miles Davis. If you can find a felt hat that can be steamed and stretched to a laughable peak, your presence will be requested — requested outside, and the doors locked behind you!

22. Water Balloon Launcher

Ancient water balloon launchers were comprised of a basket of bent ash wood and a net of supple deer hide strips. Early men would use them to practise hitting beasts large and small when their larders were filled but they still felt like hunting. There was probably a secret practice spot, and the call would often be heard, "To the cave, guys! Come on, Lascaux!"

You can make your own water balloon launcher by finding a nice slingshot-style stick in your nearest twig pile. Whittle one side of the long end flat and screw it to the end of the hockey stick, reinforcing the joint with a quick application of hockey tape or duct tape. Cut a length of nylon cord to tie across the open end of Y, creating a triangle. You can keep the cut end of the nylon cord from fraying by briefly holding it in a flame. This melted nylon burns like the dickens if it gets on you, so be careful. Use more cord to weave a nice basket-style sling. Be creative. Any tool of mayhem is appreciated in refined company if it's made well; make yours well, and you will be the envy of . . . some.

This launcher is a useful tool in the study of terminal velocities, stress loads, and the evasive tactics of those unwilling to get drenched.

Any similarities between this water balloon launcher and the traditional lacrosse stick are purely accidental.

23. Pot Rack

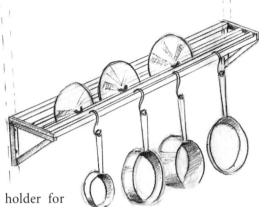

Some readers might assume that I am about to provide instructions for a handy holder for paraphernalia used in the burning of hemp. No way. I am taking the high road on this . . . uh, not that high road, the other one. These instructions are for building display space for your cooking pot collection.

A traditional pot rack, made of iron bent into graceful curves, announces that fine cooking is practised on the premises. A hockey stick pot rack screams, "Tuna melts!"

As a collection of cooking pots can be very heavy, this rack must be built strongly, so use glue and screws at all of your joints. Make your pot rack out of 36" long stick pieces so that you can easily mount it to the wall studs, which are spaced 18" apart. Cut six stick pieces and screw them together to make two triangular brackets. Securely screw the 36" stick lengths to the inside of the top piece of each bracket. If you place your slats fairly close together, you create a space across the top for the pot lids, too. Now you're ready to mount the rack by screwing the brackets into the wall studs. You may need a stud finder for this, or you could rap your knuckles along the wall until the sound changes pitch, indicating you've found the stud. Measure over 18" and you've found the next one. Use S-hooks from the hardware store to hang the pots from the rack.

24. Golf Club Rack and Rangefinder

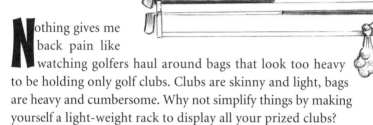

Nothing gives me back pain like watching golfers haul around bags that look too heavy to be holding only golf clubs. Clubs are skinny and light, bags are heavy and cumbersome. Why not simplify things by making yourself a light-weight rack to display all your prized clubs?

Out of four lengths of hockey stick, build a rectangular frame, making sure it is long enough to hold your longest club and wide enough to accommodate the number of clubs you'll be carrying. Next, make angled cuts in the frame's end sticks, measuring to make sure each slot is the perfect size to hold each of your clubs in place. Drill a few holes along the top just small enough to hold your golf tees snugly. Now, attach a comfortable handle to the top, and your club rack is complete. A place to carry extra golf balls? Drop six to eight balls into long sport sock, tie it to your club rack with a jaunty flourish, and you're ready to tee off.

One advantage to having a straight edge as part of your new golf rack is that you can include a handy rangefinder. Now, my understanding of the game of golf is that drinks are sometimes quaffed while on the links. Accuracy of the rangefinder may be inversely proportional to the quantity of intoxicating beverages consumed because using it demands steady nerves and the ability to wink each eye separately.

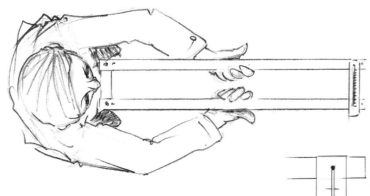

You will need two 28" lengths of stick and a crosspiece of 5", attached loosely enough to pivot, and a 2" x 6" piece of stiff card with a 1/8" by 4" slot down the centre. Four finishing nails, one at each end of the top of each stick, hammered in so about 1/4" remains above the wood, will make your "sights." On the end with the crosspiece, which will be closest to your eyes, the nails should be as far apart as your pupils. Hammer the third nail in the centre of the far end of one stick and through one end of the card. Hammer the fourth nail into the end of the other stick so that it will slide through the slot in the card. The position of the nail along the slot will be your distance indicator.

Calibrate the rangefinder by marking distances on the card. Go to a football field, and use the yard lines to work out the distances. Close one eye and sight down the nailheads to the target distance. Close that eye and sight down the other stick with the other eye at the chosen spot, without moving the first stick. Your nailhead should slide along the groove in the card. Mark where it stops, record the distance, and repeat with another yard line. The farther away the yard lines are, the wider apart the ends of the sticks will be. Parallel sticks indicate infinity. Since there are no golf courses with fairways that long yet, work down from there.

This golf club rack and rangefinder make a pretty elaborate system, but one thing is assured: you will be talked about.

25. Japanese Sandals

These will probably be the most uncomfortable sandals you've ever worn, but there must be something attractive about them because they are sold in abundance in Japan, where they are called *geta*. All you need are a bunch of hockey sticks and some fabric or soft rope to make the foot straps. If you are into big-time suffering, use scratchy hemp cord.

Determine the size before you start; the sandal should be an inch longer than the designated foot and about 5" across (5 sticks, wide side up). Any wood joined in butcher-block fashion goes together better if you run it through a joiner before glueing. Use a good wood glue and secure the soles with clamps until the glue hardens. Each sandal requires two uprights, an inch or two tall, glued and screwed onto the bottoms. Walking in these sandals requires a rocking gait, so these pieces should not be placed too close to the centre. Use a 3/8" bit to drill the thong attachment holes. Get the intended feet on the bases and mark the hole placement: one between the big toe and second toe and two back by the arch. Make a Y out of your fabric or soft rope and insert the ends into the holes in the platform, knotting them underneath to hold them in place.

If you have a streak of mischief in you, there is an alternative use for these sandals that will win your neighbours' attention and your kids' undying gratitude. Bigfoot Sandals start with oversized sandals without the uprights. Sculpt the bottoms of a huge pair of feet out of clay, paying anatomical attention to gnarled toes and cracked soles. Press an old piece of leather into the clay, then gently remove it, leaving a realistic semblance of distressed skin.

Now, make a plaster of Paris mold. Find a box slightly larger than the feet and put them sole-side up in the bottom. Brush them with liquid dishwashing soap to prevent the clay from binding with the plaster. Mix up the plaster and pour it over the clay feet. Shake the mold gently to reduce bubbles in the plaster. Let it harden. While it is setting, clean up. Don't be a duffus and pour left-over plaster down the drain. I did this as a kid, and my dad's exclamations still echo in the stratosphere.

After a couple of hours, the plaster should be set. Take the box apart, pull the clay from the plaster, and clean the remaining bits out of the cracks. These concave feet are your molds. Brush them with liquid soap and fill them with silicone caulk. Use a putty knife to get the silicone as flat as possible. Silicone may take 24 hours to set, and it is quite stinky. Sorry, you can't rush this part. Trim around each silicone foot for a realistic look and use contact cement to stick the feet to the bottoms of your oversized sandals. Attach nylon webbing so you can strap the Bigfoot Sandals to your boots. Fresh snow, not too deep, will make the best impression.

26. Library-Style Newspaper Holder

Do you remember going to an old library that had the newspapers of the day on sticks to keep them tidy and organized? The sticks rested neatly on a table or in a frame when not in use. When you took your selection to a table to read it, nobody could steal a section from you, as you were the master of that publication. You sat alone at a large table and without haste perused the day's events.

Newspapers come in several different sizes: tabloids, broadsheets, twins, doubles, and RBIs. I suggest you get your favourite journal and measure the length of it and add about 8". Now you must find lengths of hockey stick to accommodate this measurement, one for each newspaper you intend to display. Sand the edges, apply a glossy coat of varnish, and add a comfortable handle grip. To hold the papers in place, each stick will need a wire running along it just longer than the paper's gutter fold. One end should be secured with a brass screw, and at the handle end, loop the wire around another screw that holds enough tension to keep the paper on the stick. The wire will run down between the inside fold of the journal and the stick. Sound complicated?

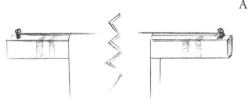

Another approach would be to make a long slot through the stick so that you could just slip the newspaper into place.

27. Kayak Hockey Stick

I have not seen a stick like this in play, but I know it is possible. An innovation so revolutionary that the game of hockey itself would be changed forever, the double-ended hockey stick must come to be! Many minutes of kayaking over the years have shown me the wisdom of such an approach: economy of motion married to smooth new technique. Playing with this amazing new hockey stick, you would never be called for high sticking, and that hook in the blade would be continually poised for belligerent action or a theatrical flourish. Sticks would no longer be right- or left-handed, they would be both. Goalies would be flummoxed by a whirling propeller-like attack. A player wielding a kayak-paddle hockey stick would make great TV — an amazing combination of Jackie Chan and Wayne Gretzky. Face-offs would have a whole new dimension, with referees ducking the twirling blades before they set the game in motion with the toss of the puck. Hockey stick manufacturers would race to re-tool and innovate further. You, however, could be there first. You could be a trend setter as you refine technique and equipment years before anyone else has a clue.

To make this stick is easy enough. Simply find two broken sticks, saw the handles of each piece at long, matching bevelled angles, clamp, screw, and glue them together. You got it.

28. Geodesic Dome

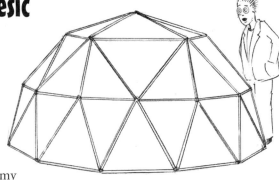

According to my meagre research, Buckminster Fuller never made a dome out of hockey sticks, undoubtedly because he was too busy inventing more things based on triangulation and explaining his name. A geodesic dome is an icosahedron, which, hellish on spellcheckers and the mathematically challenged as it may be, is simply a shape with twenty planes. Bucky (as he was called by his friends) patented the icosahedron known as the geodesic dome in the 1950s. A dark rumor persists that it was in fact first designed by the Zeiss optical company in Germany in the 1920s: the Bowlhaus School of Design, if you will.

To plan the dome, you must set aside any psychoactive components of your life because you will have to do a lot of exact measuring. Domes can be made in various sizes and complexities. For the sake of (relative) simplicity, you will work with two stick lengths. To calculate what these lengths should be, you must decide on the radius of your dome. The actual formulas used to figure out lengths and angles involves math and symbols that are so confusing I thought I was looking at a handbook dropped from a UFO. Luckily for all of us, there are several calculators that do just this on the Web — search on "Geodesic Domes, how to build."

The next problem is how to connect these sticks, and because the sticks come into many of the junctions from five different directions, the unions require a lot of fidgeting. Modern technology has come to the rescue, however: use duct tape. Sources can be found for manufactured connectors if you want a more permanent structure —

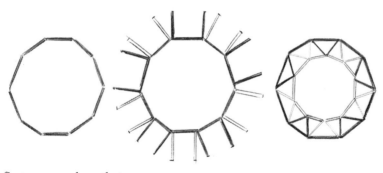

first, remember that the length of the arms of the connectors will affect the total length of the struts. But you somehow got the idea that you can make a geodesic dome with duct tape. These structures are amazingly strong, but the strength of a dome with duct tape connectors will be proportional to your taping virtuosity.

Making a geodesic dome requires sixty-five pieces of hockey stick, no matter how big a dome you want to build: 35 71-cm pieces and 30 66-cm pieces will yield a dome about 2 metres across. (Since this is science, it's all done in metric.) As you assemble the dome from the ground up, one thing will be pretty clear: you have too much time on your hands, and you need to find someone similarly gifted to assist you. Beginning with a circle made of 10 of the longer pieces, you progressively build up the dome as illustrated. It is a process of bracing, connecting, and using profanity that would make a pirate blush, but perseverance will pay off. Eventually you will have a half-sphere suitable for child's play or horseplay. Once you resume your indulgence in psychoactives (apparently a characteristic of dome dwellers), you will notice a heck of a lot of pentagons, pentagrams, and maybe even a few pentameters, depending on your stash.

29. Mock Microphone Stand

Keep this near the stereo to enhance your music-listening experience by giant steps and break any inhibitions you are harbouring. Your best times will be had with the classic R&B tunes from decades ago. You have to customize each microphone stand for the user's height as an adjusting mechanism is beyond my means to describe. I have visions of one mike for each member of the family as they sway and strut to the parade of hits, each one worthy of the Motown Hall of Fame.

As anyone who enjoys live music knows, the microphone is an essential prop to convey what a performer is really feeling. Singing with eyes closed, cradling the mike in your hand as you gaze downwards — honey, you got the blues. Holding it and your head up high so the mike is actually pointing down — hey, you WILL survive. Get in touch with the mimic within. Feel the joy and the pain of the music, right there in the comfort of your own living room. Real hockey fans might use the mock mike to do the national anthem before all televised games.

There are several options to consider. Do you need a fixed mike on a stand, suitable for back-up singers? Do you need a mike that comes off the stand for the soulful down-on-you-knees stuff? Do you need a long cord to fondle when you ask for another piece of your heart back? Get busy and find the trimmings — black rope for the cord,

electrical tape, etc. and cut your hockey sticks, the stands according to each performer's height. Use butts for the mikes. If you wish to have a mike that comes off the stand, drill a hole up into the end of it and insert and glue a piece of dowel. Then drill a hole just a bit bigger down into the top of the stand. Use electrical tape for attaching the cord to the "mike." If you intend to swing the mike energetically, tack the cord on in a few places.

The base is a little more work. It must be heavy or broad. An old hubcap with a screw through the middle from beneath into the stick might work. If you're really serious, get a large ice cream container, fill it about 4" deep with plaster of Paris, and then, before it sets, put the mike stand in the very centre. Prop it up so that it remains vertical until the plaster hardens. Once it's cured, paint the whole thing black. Deep in all our psyches lies a frustrated soul singer eager to break free. Here's your chance.

30. Lamp

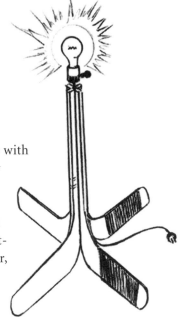

When we can't think what to do with something too good to throw away, we make a lamp out of it. Bronzed baby shoes, driftwood, old Portuguese wine bottles — all are embryonic lamps. Ludwig Wittgenstein, the Austrian philosopher, wanted us to look at the underlying nature of common things, to discover their hidden truths, in short, to deconstruct them. Turning broken hockey sticks into a lamp brings out their cultural and societal essence: the wood, the fabrication, the game, the conflict, and their demise.

This hockey stick lamp isn't just a lamp, it's a Statement, and making it gives those hockey sticks their redemption. You may choose any variant: floor lamp, table lamp, or wall lamp. Glue the shafts at the corners so the blades form a radiating pattern of 90°. This will leave a nice channel for the electrical cord. In fact, by strange coincidence, some of the newer sticks already have channels in them. You can buy the fittings at the top for the bulb and shade at a hardware store.

The lamp shade is another project entirely, but in the spirit of this artwork, try to deconstruct a shade. You can of course yield to the darker side and create a little assemblage of hockey paraphernalia, but fight the urge, unless of course the lamp is a gift for a sentimental hockey parent. In that case, give it the works.

31. Jack-o-Lantern Holder

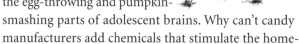

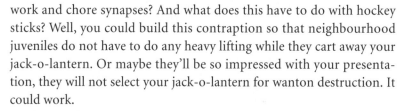

Halloween can be a problematic time. Jack-o-lanterns tend to be stolen and smashed. Youth are prone to unexpected behavioral shifts when gorging on refined sugar, and adults feed the frenzy. All that candy must stimulate the egg-throwing and pumpkin-smashing parts of adolescent brains. Why can't candy manufacturers add chemicals that stimulate the home-work and chore synapses? And what does this have to do with hockey sticks? Well, you could build this contraption so that neighbourhood juveniles do not have to do any heavy lifting while they cart away your jack-o-lantern. Or maybe they'll be so impressed with your presentation, they will not select your jack-o-lantern for wanton destruction. It could work.

This holder is based on an easy configuration of three sticks of identical length. You must tie them relatively loosely at the centre and spread the ends out so that the pumpkin fits in the cradle shape. If the centre is secure enough, your structure will be pretty stable. If it isn't, it will come crashing down, and you will not have to wait for the vandals. A pair of these flanking your front door on Hallowe'en night gives a nice balance to your decor.

Your holder has other than merely decorative uses, too. A triangular piece of waterproof cloth with slots cut out for the sticks to go through makes a dandy bird bath for the yard, or even a portable sink for when you go camping.

32. Ice Croquet Set

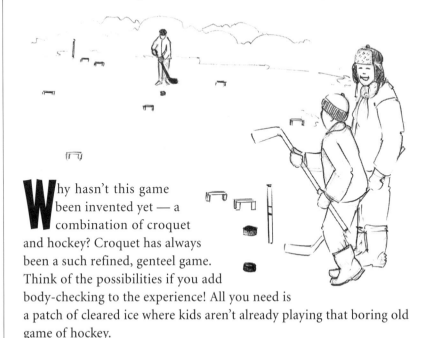

Why hasn't this game been invented yet — a combination of croquet and hockey? Croquet has always been a such refined, genteel game. Think of the possibilities if you add body-checking to the experience! All you need is a patch of cleared ice where kids aren't already playing that boring old game of hockey.

Now for the equipment. The wickets must be made sturdily, using glue and screws. Make them tall enough to allow a puck to pass through. Each player's puck should have a different colour of paint dabbed on the surface for identification purposes. You will need nine wickets, but make extra in case there is just too much exuberance once the trinity of ice, puck, and stick come together. For the end posts, you can use more hockey sticks. Insert a double-ended screw into the bottom of each and screw them directly into the ice.

Setting the game up will require some real planning. Lawn croquet merely calls for firm insertion of the wickets into the ground, but that won't work on ice. Nailing in the wickets might meet with protest from other skaters. And the wickets must be secure enough to withstand those banking ricochet shots. So you'll need to make bases for your ice wickets by screwing on pieces of thin plastic cut from the lids

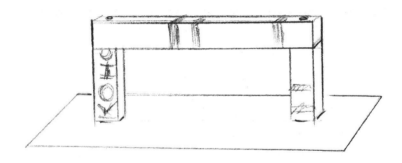

of ice cream containters. Then the bases can be frozen securely to the ice surface, possibly in the dark. Do your watering at night, the customary time for hauling out the hose and freezing your fingers to numb nubs, and you'll be ready for a fast-paced game of ice croquet in the morning.

The game is played the same way as croquet, only with hockey sticks and pucks. Same rules, except you don't get that very satisfying "thwunk" that you get in the lawn version when hitting a competitor's croquet ball out of your way.

33. Windmill

Hockey and windmills both are associated with characters named Don, who charge about with their sidekicks while loudly spouting opinions. In this spirit, I feel it is appropriate to provide you with instructions to make a windmill out of hockey sticks.

A windmill requires an efficient rotating device. A bicycle wheel is perfect. It's okay to venture in this direction because of a precedent set by an artistic Frenchman named Marcel Duchamp who placed ready-mades like urinals and shovels on pedestals, thereby taking art in a new direction. Duchamp made appropriation respectable. So feel to free appropriate a bicycle wheel for your project.

The long, graceful curve of the hockey stick is perfect for the old-fashioned windmill look of Iberian landscapes. You will need six to eight sticks cut to the same length. Drill holes in the sticks so you can wire them to the inside of the bike wheel at the rim and hub. Before you start wiring, make sure the blades are all facing the same direction. Secure the sticks, evenly spaced, with the blades in line and the wide side of the sticks against the rim. Use pliers to get the wire good and tight.

Now you will need some fabric. Use an old sheet that is destined for the rag bag. Cut the cloth into long right-angle triangles with bases the length of the hockey stick blades, the straight sides the length of the sticks, and tapering to a point where the stick end is attached to the wheel hub. If you hem each edge, your windmill will last longer and be stronger. Staple the fabric along the stick, from blade to end, leaving the longest edge of the fabric free to catch the wind. The cloth should be pretty taut, but not so taut that it rips.

Of course, the trick with wind-mills is that they need to rotate into the wind. You already have a nice bolt sticking out of the back of that bike wheel, so you can fit that easily into an L bracket. You should affix this to a two-by-four which is equipped with a base and a roller bearing, kind of like what you find on an office chair. Don't strip apart office chairs though — see what the hardware store has to offer.

It is easy to make this windmill for purely decorative purposes. If, however, you insist on a practical application, such as lifting water or making electricity, you're on your own. You will have to figure out a way to affix a pulley mechanism to the spokes and then attach that to your functional device. And that's way too complex for me.

34. Stilts

Stilts are a welcome addition to any kid's pile of junk in the shed. They are loads of fun, but because you are using broken hockey sticks, you might have to make short stilts. The longest hockey stick allowed by the NHL is 63". Given that your sticks are broken somewhere short of that length, you will be making stilts for short people. The sticks must be of equal length and long enough for the user to hook his elbows around.

A good footrest is mandatory for stilts to function properly. A wedge cut from a two-by-four makes a fine platform. Screw it on from the outside of the hockey stick through to the centre of the wedge. Use several screws on each footrest.

Have you ever seen those stilt-walkers who dress up like Abraham Lincoln? This could be you. All you need is a very long pair of pants, practice, and a parade. Imagine yourself tripping down Main Street, falling from great heights, tumbling into the marching band, landing on a majorette, and the town paper captures it all on film and uses it on the front page, while your children shun you for buffoonery and run-on sentences! Imagine! In this spirit, I won't tell you how to make these potentially embarrassing parade stilts. Stilts are more of a back yard endeavour, anyway. And the addition of a sharp point protruding from the bottom would enable you to aerate your lawn while practicing!

35. Puck Display Shelf

Many pucks lost in the snow-banks around frozen ponds or lakes slowly drift to the bottom in a gentle, tumbling descent with the spring thaw. There they lie forever, inert rubber, dark and forgotten. There is no need, however, to forget those prized pucks that never quite get into circulation. You know, the souvenir pucks with the colourful team logos. They could be displayed on the wall in your hand-made puck display shelf. You require but an old hockey stick and a sabre saw.

First find a long piece of hockey stick. You will need to space out your pucks evenly along the length of your stick. After the spacing issues are resolved, you must mark your cutting lines along the stick. Make your-self a template by drawing a straight line across the face of an old puck about 1/2" from the bottom edge. Place this line against the top of your mounting stick and mark your cutting lines, creating a series of consistent scallops in which to rest your pucks. Use two C clamps to secure the stick to your work table, with the area to be cut well over the edge. Cut carefully, and then sand the cut areas smooth. Secure to the wall with finishing nails and insert your puck collection in the slots. You now have a ready supply of hard rubber things to throw at mice or other unwelcome guests.

36. Trellis

An artist's greatest fear is to see his work offered at a yard sale for three dollars and nobody seems remotely interested except another artist who buys it strictly for the material to make canvas stretchers. The sentient hockey stick's greatest fear is to become a tomato stake — the bottom rung of busted-hockey-stick transformation. I beg you not to subject a retired and disfigured staff to such humiliation. Make a trellis. Transform those pieces of wood into a classic garden embellishment. In one afternoon of sawing, measuring, cussing, measuring again, sawing some more, hammering, cussing, and digging, you can have this attractive trellis finished and your wife pleading, "Please put it somewhere else." Take no notice, craftsmen of the world. You are an artist and deserve your entrance to the salon. Are you a mere *refusé*? Stand tall and put that trellis where the world can see it! Those subtle accents and finely trimmed angles speak of Old World traditions

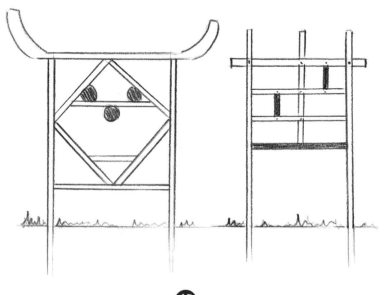

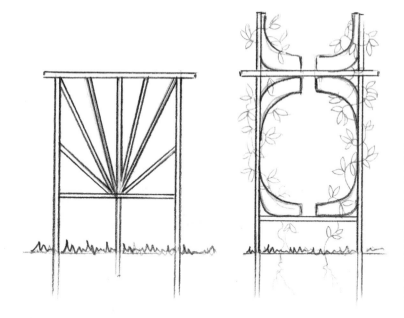

(possibly the ones that put your ancestors on a boat, exiled for sloppy workmanship.) Should you care to paint over old logos on the sticks for the sake of harmony of hue, the world will take even more notice. Imagine a British racing green grid, entwined with climbing roses and splashed with red and white blooms. You get the picture. As for the harmony of hue, well, I've never heard hue sing.

As anyone in the snow belt knows, a frost heave is not what happens when you eat your Freezie too quickly. Nope, it's that unpredictable ground shifting in the spring that sets foundations, patios, and yes, trellises askew. I have been told that a footing of 36" below ground level is necessary. That's some long hockey sticks you'll be needing!

37. GPS (Global Positioning Stick)

A brand new electronic GPS goes for hundreds of dollars, but this one won't set you back anything. Using just a hockey stick, a protractor, an accurate clock, and a paper clip on a string, you can locate yourself about as accurately as a 15th-century explorer could.

Knowing your place in the world takes years. Finding your place in the world requires only that you know which way is north. Knowing north, you can find your latitude — the theoretical parallel lines measured in degrees from the equator (0°) to the poles (90° north or south). Finding your longitude — the theoretical lines running from pole to pole around the planet (360°) — is a bit trickier, but anything is possible with a busted hockey stick.

This Global Positioning Stick (GPS) requires a clear view of Polaris (the North Star). Polaris never moves in the northern sky; it sits over the north pole. If you see it low on the horizon, you don't need to worry about snow storms, but you'll pay big bucks for ice time because you're near the equator. The higher Polaris is in the sky, the further north you are. To get your declination, tape a protractor to the edge of your hockey stick, with the 90° mark at the centre of the stick. Tie or tape a string weighted with a paper clip to the flat edge of the protractor at the 90° mark. The string and clip should hang free at 0° when the stick is horizontal. As you sight along the stick towards Polaris, take a reading of the angle the string crosses. Do this several times and average the readings. This is your latitude; it will be somewhere between 0° and 90°.

Finding longitude is tougher. You must know the exact times of sunrise and sunset. Measure how many hours of daylight you have, or find that information in the newspaper, and divide those daylight hours by two. This is midday, when you will take your readings. Plant a length of straight hockey stick vertically on a flat surface. A few minutes before midday, go out and take readings of the stick's shadow every five minutes. At the point where the shadow is smallest, note the time. This is your midday reading. Now find out what time it is in Greenwich, England, when it's midday here. You cannot figure this out with a hockey stick unless you are beyond clever, but a newspaper or internet inquiry will work. The time zones of the world are based on the location of the observatory in Greenwich, England, and an atlas will show how many time zones from Greenwich you are. Add this number to your midday time. Now subtract the time of midday in Greenwich. Convert the left-over minutes to decimals. Multiply this whole thing by 15 (360° divided by 24 time zones). This is your longitude.

And there you have it: your exact position on the earth, determined by a broken hockey stick.

38. Hat Rack

If you collect baseball hats, this project is for you. You will need a lot of hockey stick blades. Any self-respecting hockey player will tell you that some blades curve left and others right. An aesthetic decision must be made, therefore, as to the arrangement of the blades. I would suggest an equal number of blades of each orientation, mounted so that they curve outward from the middle towards each end. If you were a fine arts major in university, you could say, "The confluence of the organic bend of each curve speaks of the interplay of structure and utility. It is a didactic representation of a neo-postmodern adaptation to form." Now, how you explain your ridiculous collection of baseball hats is up to you. You must cut consistently exact angles at the handle end of the blades so they all project at the same pitch. If you are not confident in your ability to measure such precise angles, you can forego the blades and just use sawed-off 6" hockey stick pieces as pegs for the hats.

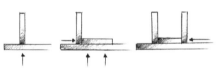

→ = SCREW PLACEMENT

To create this fine hat rack, find a piece of stick longer than the desired width of the finished rack to use as the mounting piece. Cut each peg 5" long, and cut 4" pieces as spacers to fit between the pegs. (So, for example, if you have 5 pegs you will need 4 spacers.) Lay out the rack before assembling. Leave 2" on each end and place the pegs and spacers accordingly. Drill a hole in each end for your mounting hardware. A fine embellishment would a fancy rink-rat-style taping job to make a knob at the end of each peg, thereby improving their grip. Do this before you attach the pegs to the back. Start assembling by drilling and screwing the first peg from the back of the rack. Screw on the first spacer from behind with two screws, making sure it fits tightly against the peg. Put another screw through the peg into the spacer. Repeat the process with each peg.

39. Shoe Horn

Kids these days just don't respect their shoes. I can't even get my kids to untie their laces when they take their shoes off, and putting them on involves grinding the cuff of a still-tied shoe with the heel until the footwear obliges. Even in today's world of wonder materials, sooner rather than later the shoe wilts. The back of the shoe, whose parts are known in the business as the quarter and the outside counter, become a flattened, sorry mess. Curiously, my kids would never wear shoes that cost a quarter or were bought at an outside counter.

The busted hockey stick can help. If you carve out the flat side of the end of a hockey stick, you can make a shoehorn — the perfect tool to halt the traumatization of footwear in your house.

Shoehorns have a rounded base thin enough to slip out of the shoe once your foot is in. For this reason, I suggest you use a laminated hockey stick,

as solid wood might be too brittle. The smoother you get the wood, the better it works. You will need to sand it down, splinter free, to about 1/8" inch thickness. It need not be varnished, but the smoother you sand it, the happier your feet, socks, and shoes will be.

40. Ribbon Dance Baton

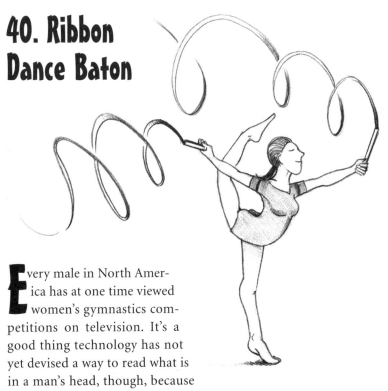

Every male in North America has at one time viewed women's gymnastics competitions on television. It's a good thing technology has not yet devised a way to read what is in a man's head, though, because there is just something about young, fit women doing contortions and splits that brings on thoughts best left trailing off to dots . . .

During these competitions, there is one truly wacky activity. The gymnasts set about twirling and leaping with a long ribbon apparatus. I suggest China as the origin of this activity, solely because I've often seen svelte characters in James Bond movies carrying on with this apparatus when the scene moves near the Great Wall. On the other hand, it could have been devised by a foppish bull-whipper, for all I know. My suspicion is that when the big cull starts, eliminating arcane and silly events from the Olympics, this "dance of the ribbons" will top many lists. Don't let this be an impediment, however, to crafting your own ribbon geegaws, which are customarily made with broken hockey sticks. Many of those gymnast babes have big burly hockey-player boyfriends who gladly share the splintered tools of their trade. These fragments of manliness, uh, I guess I mean broken hockey sticks here, are cleaved, sanded, and dandified. Voila! Ribbon dance batons.

You know you need yet another broken hockey stick. Have you reached the bottom of the pile yet? You only need two pieces about 12" long. Now paint them purple, or how about chartreuse? You could wrap them in colourful ribbon, or, better yet, create a truly inspired design in hockey stick tape. You need to attach those long ribbons to one end of each baton, preferably three of them, about 12' long. You will be amazed at how expensive ribbon is, so maybe some "do not enter — crime scene" tape can be borrowed, unnoticed, from the local constabulary. Use tacks to attach the ribbons to the ends of the sticks, making sure to cover the tacks with ribbon or tape for a nicely finished look. Put on your favorite music and release that gymnast within.

41. Action Figure

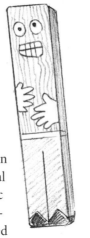

The busted hockey stick action figure can be fabricated in several styles. The easiest is the basic Stickman. This requires the most imagination and might get the puzzled looks only young innocents can attain. A quick application of markers (heaven forbid you should bother to paint the thing) will provide basic anatomical clues. Since it takes less than a minute to make one, you might as well make a bunch of them and overwhelm the kiddies with sheer volume.

You might wish to advance to the with-arms model. Big, clunky arms as wide as the torso — does that look right? Of course not, you need to cut the stick pieces down to size. A scroll saw or band saw works well. If you're really motivated, you could cut the arms at the elbows and articulate them. Hinge the elbows with a bit of leather. If you are thinking of fingers, you're way beyond me. Legs can be fashioned in the same manner with big, clunky boots glued and tacked to the ends. When it comes to making the head, I find the no-neck look creates a real no-neck hero.

If you have a lot of broken hockey sticks and a lot of time on your hands, then you should consider the BIG ONE. Make a hockey-themed chess set. The team owners are king and queen, coaches are knights, refs are bishops, and corporate sponsors are the castles. The players are, of course, the pawns.

42. Door Knocker

Imagine the amount of electricity consumed by the millions of door bells being rung every minute around the world. Why, global warming is being accelerated immeasurably by this button-pushing cacophony. Save the planet. Make a door knocker out of a broken hockey stick!

Most manual door knockers operate under the "pendulum interrupted" principle. A mass swings on a pivot in an arc, and instead of gracefully climbing against gravity, it smashes into a door. A nice sounding board and mounting plate keep to a minimum any damage by enthusiastic salesmen.

The decision about what to use as a weight at the end of your door knocker is pretty open ended. The fact that a broken hockey stick will be your knocker arm is a given. What must be considered, however, is that you need a darned good collision of solid objects to transmit a vibration that will alert those inside to a visitor. You need something with heft. You could invoke the patron saint of unnecessary mechanisms, Rube Goldberg. Using his design philosophy, you could easily empty that hockey kit bag in the name of astounding those coming to your front door. If you are really stymied by all this, you could just leave a hockey stick by the front door with a sign: "Rap sharply to announce your presence."

43. CD Holder

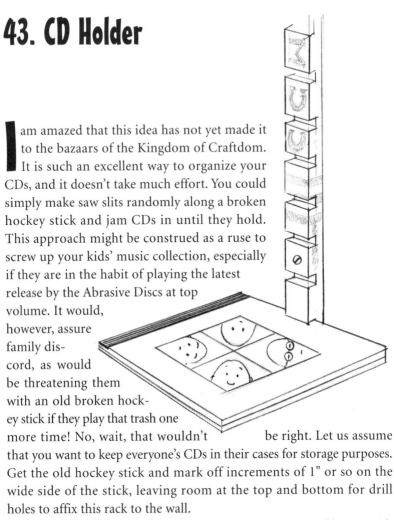

I am amazed that this idea has not yet made it to the bazaars of the Kingdom of Craftdom. It is such an excellent way to organize your CDs, and it doesn't take much effort. You could simply make saw slits randomly along a broken hockey stick and jam CDs in until they hold. This approach might be construed as a ruse to screw up your kids' music collection, especially if they are in the habit of playing the latest release by the Abrasive Discs at top volume. It would, however, assure family dis-cord, as would be threatening them with an old broken hock-ey stick if they play that trash one more time! No, wait, that wouldn't be right. Let us assume that you want to keep everyone's CDs in their cases for storage purposes. Get the old hockey stick and mark off increments of 1" or so on the wide side of the stick, leaving room at the top and bottom for drill holes to affix this rack to the wall.

Now, here is where you'll need to know how to use a table saw with a dado blade. These blades take out wood in paths instead of slits. Get someone to help you if this is new territory. Set the blade for 7/16", just wide enough to hold a CD case securely. Set up a guide or block so that you will saw the same depth into the stick each time. Repetitive motion breeds dangerous reflection. Your mind drifts to a weekend evening, the kids are fast asleep, you've just watched a really hot movie. PAY ATTENTION! You are operating a power tool.

After the slots are cut and the mounting holes drilled, it's time to resolve the to-paint-or-not-to-paint issue. Neatly sanded and painted, your CD holder will resemble the offerings of a certain Scandinavian decorating store that would have sold it to you for at least five dollars. A glossy primary colour would be nice, unless you live in Toronto, where by law you must paint it black to match your wardrobe. Finally, it's time to mount the holder. Use a level, find a stud, put it up. If your household is like mine, of course, certain additions to the decor must be cleared though proper channels — especially if this is an addition to wall space in a common area frequented by visitors, family, and the like.

44. Weather Vane

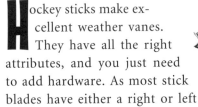

ockey sticks make ex-cellent weather vanes. They have all the right attributes, and you just need to add hardware. As most stick blades have either a right or left curve, your weather vane can be asymmetrical, or you can use a couple of screws to affix an identical stick with the opposite curve to give your weather vane the chicken-tail look. The "stabiliser" or blade of the stick will catch the wind and swing the point of the stick directly into the wind. The "indicator" end of the stick should be carved and sanded to a nice point. A brass pointer fixed over the end would look classy. If you are a true wizard of artisanry, consider as ornamentation a hammered copper rendition of Ken Dryden fending off the north wind.

A weather vane pivots along a horizontal axis, so you need to set up a system to allow yours to swing with the wind. Wind vanes usually pivot on a pin that swivels in a tube filled with grease. A really long nail of the kind used to hang rain gutters will make a good pin. Using a bit the same diameter as the nail, drill a hole through the stick, top to bottom, half-way between tail and tip. Put the nail through this hole, adding some glue or epoxy to hold it firmly in place. Now comes the tricky part. If this is to be a true wind vane set up on your roof, I suggest that you retain the services of a metalworker who will make the tube that holds the pin and also the bracket that screws onto the roof, which is bolted to the tube. Over the years, these instruments of wind indication go through a lot of stress. You need tough hardware. Metalworkers are familiar with these set-ups and can manufacture you a custom-made gizmo. When you are installing the wind vane on the roof, pay attention. You don't need extra holes up there; it is a roof, after all. Install it over the eaves, or attach it to the chimney. Now stand back and get downwind from all those compliments.

Here's the truly tacky version. Duct tape an old skate to a broken stick, and put an old hockey glove over the other end, with the stick in the index finger of the glove. Tape the glove to the stick. Drill the stick and add the pin, as above, and duct tape the nail head. Drill a block of wood with a bit slightly larger than the nail, throw some grease in the hole, insert the pin, and you're done. You now have a weather vane worthy of a last minute science fair project. You will score high on laughs, low on science.

45. Guitar Stand

Guitars should never be left leaning up against sofas, bookshelves, or wherever smarty-pants art directors place them in the set-up for a casual photo shoot. A guitar belongs in its case or on a guitar stand. And if you have a bunch of shorter lengths of hockey stick around, then you are in luck. You can make a guitar stand that is both functional and unique.

The stand should be at least 18" high. The vertical shafts should lean about 5° back of perpendicular, as the guitar will be more secure if it reclines a little. The base sticks should be at least 10" to 12" long for stability. Guitars come in a wide range of thicknesses, so cut your support pieces accordingly. Install a good quality cabinet hinge at the crux of the sticks. Use plenty of tape around this area. Your guitar back rests here and needs a non-abrasive surface. Pieces of bicycle inner tube wrapped around the places where the guitar touches the stand will eliminate any worry about sliding (remove the valve stem, of course). You could use hockey tape, but it may have adhesive residue on the top side. It's your call. A string across the span of the vertical pieces will prevent the stand from collapsing, or you could use a length of stick. This is a funky-looking guitar stand, but rest assured, it's a true one-of-a-kind.

46. Hobby Horse

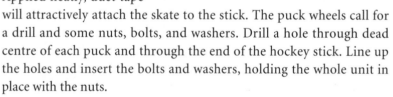

The curve of the blade of a hockey stick has a refined equine profile. Okay, maybe not at first glance, but once you add some ears, paint on some eyes and a nose, and attach a halter, you'll be saying "Giddyap, pardner!" For a real customized look, you can add a saddle made out of an old skate boot and puck wheels at the base. Applied neatly, duct tape will attractively attach the skate to the stick. The puck wheels call for a drill and some nuts, bolts, and washers. Drill a hole through dead centre of each puck and through the end of the hockey stick. Line up the holes and insert the bolts and washers, holding the whole unit in place with the nuts.

As a point of interest, the original hobby horse was developed by the ancient Klucks as a ploy to outwit the Myopians at the Battle of Smutz. The Myopians were bad at finding and saddling up their own horses, so the steeds did not take commands well. The Klucks, on the other hand, were horseless yet clever. A quick Kluckian carpenter evaluated their situation and their resources, (large supplies of broken hockey sticks) and the hobby horse was born. The outwitted Myopians surmised they were indeed goners and gave up their steeds in defeat. The discarded faux horses became the playthings of young Klucks and eventually children everywhere. How this got to be a hobby is anyone's guess.

47. Backpack

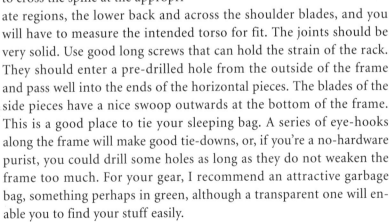

You would think that a backpack made out of broken hockey sticks would be pretty uncomfortable. That would be an astute and correct observation. If you are heading out on the Appalachian Trail and have something to prove with hockey sticks, however, it's easy to manufacture a rig that will not make a hockey veteran suffer beyond the level of acceptability.

It's essential for the framework to cross the spine at the appropriate regions, the lower back and across the shoulder blades, and you will have to measure the intended torso for fit. The joints should be very solid. Use good long screws that can hold the strain of the rack. They should enter a pre-drilled hole from the outside of the frame and pass well into the ends of the horizontal pieces. The blades of the side pieces have a nice swoop outwards at the bottom of the frame. This is a good place to tie your sleeping bag. A series of eye-hooks along the frame will make good tie-downs, or, if you're a no-hardware purist, you could drill some holes as long as they do not weaken the frame too much. For your gear, I recommend an attractive garbage bag, something perhaps in green, although a transparent one will enable you to find your stuff easily.

Make shoulder straps from a wide piece of nylon webbing. For strength, double it over where you secure it to the frame. If you don't want to purchase webbing, you can cut up lengths of bicycle inner tube, but cut off the valve stem so it won't worm its way into your flesh. If the straps must be adjustable, you will have to buy buckles from a fabric or backpacking store. A waist strap will balance the load. Use something you can tie, or buy a buckle.

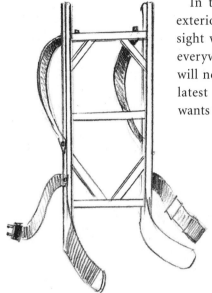

In the latest camping catalogues, exterior frame packs are nowhere in sight while internal frame packs are everywhere. Your hockey stick pack will never be seen in a review of the latest outdoor equipment, but who wants to be a slave to fashion?

48. Pooper Scooper

The laws of urban decorum no longer allow us to let our dogs crap any where they want to. Most municipalities have a poop-and-scoop law, but I find something distasteful about doing the inverted plastic bag trick which gives me a handful of warm dog poop just one polymer-width away from my skin. At least with a pooper scooper, you can fling your dog's evacuations wildly into some unpopulated area, should you care to.

To make this handy tool, fit an old skate to the blade end of a hockey stick with a careful but vigorous application of hockey tape. You're done.

Note that the top of a skate has good stiff support. This is such a perfect turd lifter that MIT couldn't design one better. You also have a perfect reservoir to hold the accumulation. Once the skate is filled, however, the emptying business must be attended to — the location of which will test the depths of your depravity. The tongue of the skate, unfortunately, is often padded with rather absorbent material. In fact, a long-term application of this tool is not without accompanying odors and cleaning problems. You will want to store this thing outside.

A dignified tool this will be, too, since from a distance nobody will suspect that you are hauling a pooper scooper; you will just look like you are taking your dog to the rink.

49. Massage Wheel

We have all seen those holistic hard wood massage thinga-majigs that are sold at scented soap stores. They look vaguely Scandinavian. If the promise of an encounter with one of these has you enthralled, let me tell you how to make your very own out of a broken hockey stick and two pucks.

Cut a length of hockey stick to about 18", and then find two pucks with only a few chinks on the edges. Get a 1/8" bolt 3" long with a self-locking nut. Place each puck against a wide side of the handle. Then drill a hole through all three components at dead centre of the pucks and 1" up from the bottom of the handle, making sure the hole is slightly bigger than the bolt. Washers placed between the pucks and the wood will make for easy rolling. So will a little wax or soap rubbed on the part of the bolt that goes through the wood. If you smooth the pucks off to a nicely rounded edge, you might actually get invited to put this thing to work on the spine of someone you care about.

Remember, the spine is an amazing collection of 24 vertebrae, the principal function of which is to protect the core of nerves that run up the centre. This conglomeration of bone and flexible discs goes unnoticed when all is hunky dory, but, when things get wonky, we are not happy. In this spirit, I counsel you not to use this puck-rolling massager on a back that is hurting.

50. Marimba

An outdoor hockey game fills the air with shouts of joy and the swoosh of skates. Why not add something else? Make a marimba out of hockey sticks to enhance the soundtrack at the local frozen pond with the trill of a calypso tune. Marimbas are just pieces of wood, precisely cut and assembled, that resonate over a chamber of air. You have those broken hockey sticks that look curiously like wide piano keys when cut down to length. You just need some metal tubing for resonators, some metal bar, and music lessons.

A typical marimba will have 37 bars (keys), including the sharps and flats, providing three octaves. The lowest and highest notes are C. Striking a key sends a column of vibrating air down the tube below, and the length of this vibrating column of air gives pitch. The shorter the bar and tube, the higher the note, and the longer the bar and tube, the lower the note. The shortest key will be about 3 1/2" long, and the longest key will be about 6". The length of the resonating tubes depends on the tube diameter.

Find four metal rods about 3/8" in diameter and the length of the keyboard. Look for something that will not bend when the tubes are suspended from it. Two of these rods run through each bar, and you will have two rows of bars, one for whole tones and the other for semitones,

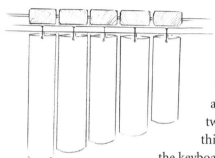

like a piano keyboard. The holes you drill through the bars should be slightly larger than the rod so each bar can vibrate independently from the adjoining bars. Felt spacers between the bars will help maintain this independence and improve the keyboard appearance.

All the resonating tubes will be different lengths. To add them to the marimba, start with the lowest note. Cut a length of tubing that you think would be about right. Near the top, drill 2 holes exactly opposite each other. Pass a string through these holes and suspend the tube beneath the centre of the longest bar and as close to the bar as possible. File a little notch into the rod to keep the string in place. Get near a piano or electronic keyboard and plonk on the bar over the end of the tube. Keep shortening the tube until you're as close to C below middle C as possible. (Of course, if the tube is already too short, use it for another note and cut a longer piece of tubing for the lowest one.) That's one note out of the way, 36 more to go.

When you're done, you will be desperately looking for something to set the marimba on. You need to make a frame. Hockey sticks to the rescue. Legs? Hockey sticks. Mallets? Hockeysticks!

Index

Notes

Notes

Peter Manchester is an accomplished illustrator and painter whose youthful tinkering was a true test of his parents' affection. They did their best to keep him away from the influence of hockey in Belgium, the Congo, France, Norway, and finally the United States. There he tried his hand at many trades, including ski bum, newspaper reporter, and museum curator. He arrived in the land of real ice in 1992 and settled in Sackville, New Brunswick.

A serendipitous encounter with his son's broken hockey sticks unleashed a torrent of ideas. In the face of incredulity and amazement, this Leonardo of Laminated Sticks stretched the bounds of glue, duct tape, good taste, and craftsmanship to write and illustrate his first book, *50 Things to Make with a Broken Hockey Stick*. He is currently combing Sackville yard sales and hockey rinks for even more broken sticks with which to fabricate the fantastic creations of the future.

Visit Peter Manchester's web site at www.petermanchester.ca.